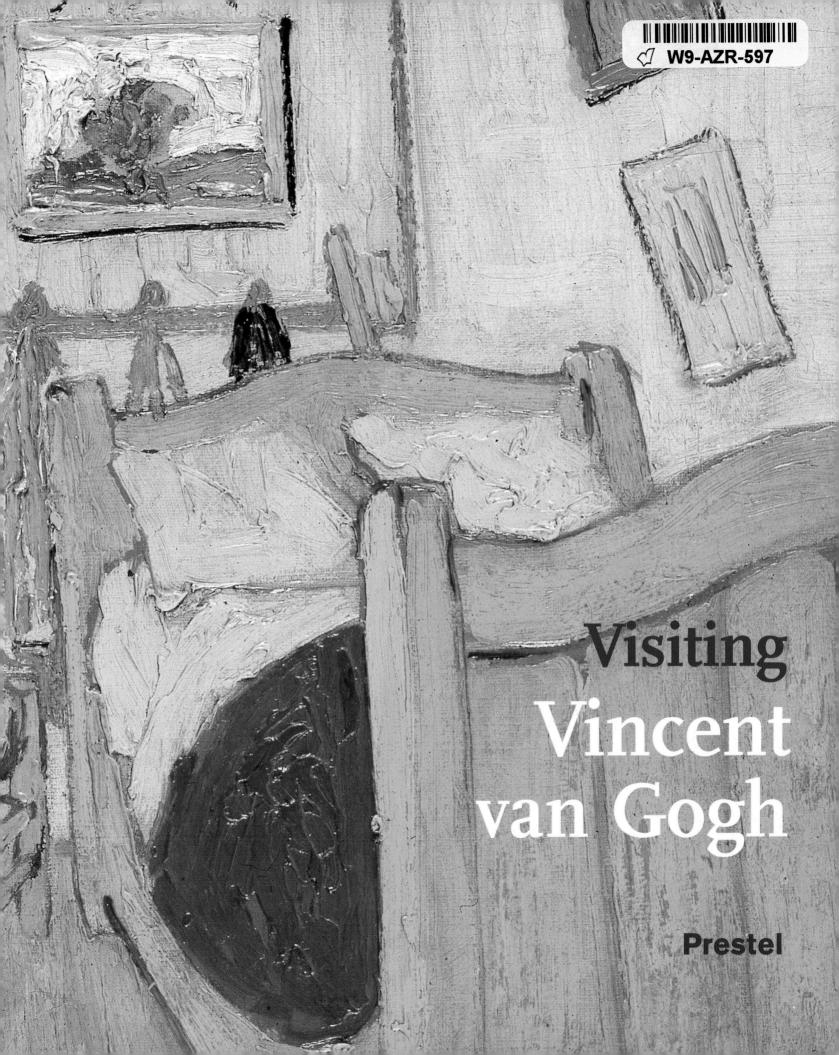

Visiting
Vincent
van Gogh

Prestel

Here is a man. He is painting.

In his hand he has a palette with different colours:
Orange, Blue, Red, Green and Yellow,

and several brushes, one for each colour.
The man has red hair and a red beard.
He is looking at us seriously with dark eyes.

ho is this man?

He is the painter Vincent van Gogh.

Vincent van Gogh was born in Holland in 1853. At the age of 16 he started work. At first he was employed in his Uncle Cent's art shop in The Hague. After that he wanted to become a teacher, and then a clergyman, like his father. But he didn't like any of these jobs and, in 1880, when he was 27 years old, he decided to devote all his time to art. From this point on, he wanted only to draw and paint.

He made a lot of effort and worked hard, because he had made up his mind to make a career as an artist. And so he drew, sketched and painted everything he saw: animals, landscapes, houses and other things, but mainly people. And most of all, simple country folk.

This is one of those pictures of a farming family. Van Gogh painted them having their evening meal. They are eating potatoes and drinking coffee.

It is dark in the room because there is only one lamp.

The hands of these people are large, and you can tell by looking at them that they have to work hard every day.

In sketches like these, van Gogh practised drawing hands.

Van Gogh was very proud of this picture. He thought that after many years of practice, he had finally succeeded in creating a really good painting.

Now he was a real artist!

After van Gogh had lived for a while in Holland and had painted many country folk, he became restless.
He wanted to experience more and especially to find out more about art.
His brother Theo, who was 4 years younger, had been living in Paris for some years.
In his letters he told Vincent a lot about the French city, where the Eiffel Tower was just being built, and about the many artists who lived there.

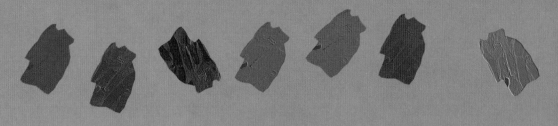

Full of curiosity, Vincent joined Theo in Paris in 1886. The Parisian artists he met didn't paint such dark paintings of poor farmers, but colourful, cheerful pictures. Van Gogh liked this and he also turned to bright, glowing colours.

Vincent's brother, Theo van Gogh

The picture on the right shows Julien Tanguy, who sold paintings and paints and whom van Gogh affectionately called "père" (father). Père Tanguy lived in Paris and knew many artists. He helped them to sell their works and was one of the few people who admired van Gogh's paintings. In this portrait he is looking down with a kind expression. Behind him there are a lot of pictures! They are Japanese works of art, because, when van Gogh lived in Paris, Japanese art and culture were very fashionable there. Vincent and Theo collected Japanese pictures and Vincent took to painting Japanese women and landscapes.

6

Although van Gogh learned a lot in Paris, experimenting with his style and improving his technique, he remained restless. In 1888 he moved to the peaceful, warm south of France, to the town of Arles. In Arles van Gogh lived in this yellow house on the corner with the green shutters. A man is just walking past it. Has he been visiting van Gogh? Perhaps it is even the artist himself, who is popping over to the café with the pink awning to get something to eat? The woman in the blue skirt is already greeting him.

Shall we secretly have a look inside his house while the painter is not at home ?

8

We are now in Vincent van Gogh's bedroom.

Careful, the floor crrrreaks!

y the wall stands a wooden bed and next to it a table and two chairs.
Some jackets and a yellow hat are hanging on the coat pegs.
You can see pictures on the walls: two portraits, a landscape with a tree and two drawings on
white paper. On the left there is a mirror next to the window. The shutters are closed.

9

Let's leave his room and go for a walk together with van Gogh through the town of Arles.

Look, there is the man with the long beard, Joseph Roulin, the postman — he can easily be recognised by his uniform and his cap. Van Gogh and Roulin greet each other warmly, they are good friends. In this picture we can see how van Gogh has painted Roulin in front of a background of cheerful flowers.

10

He also painted his wife, Augustine Roulin. Five times, to be exact. He gave one of these paintings to Mrs. Roulin as a present.

Van Gogh called this painting of Mrs. Roulin *La Berceuse*, which means "Lullaby". He wrote this title on the painting as well, on the right next to the chair. We can tell that the woman is sitting in front of a cradle by the rope she is holding in her hand. Can you imagine what the rope is for?

It's fastened to the cradle and when Mrs. Roulin pulls it a little, the cradle keeps rocking. The flowered wallpaper in the background looks exactly like that in the picture of the postman, Roulin. Do you think van Gogh painted these portraits in the Roulin's home?

11

If we go a bit further, some way outside the town to the south we come to the
wooden drawbridge of Réginelle. Van Gogh named it the Bridge of Langlois.
A horse-drawn carriage is travelling across the bridge and on the river-bank
women with white caps on their heads are doing their washing in the river.
Near them a half-sunken boat lies on the bank.
Van Gogh seemed to like this bridge very much and painted it several times.

When we come back to the town it is evening.
But it is warm and people are still sitting on the terrace of the café.

13

Van Gogh had a dream. He wanted to live and work together with other artists in his yellow house in Arles. So he invited the artist Paul Gauguin, whom he had met in Paris, to come to him in Arles.

To decorate the guest-room for Gauguin, van Gogh painted some pictures of cheerful, yellow sunflowers, like the ones which bloom all around the town of Arles in August and September.

Van Gogh was enchanted by the different yellow and gold colours he saw in the flowers and he thought that only a very talented artist would be able to capture all these colours in a painting.

Paul Gauguin
Van Gogh Painting Sunflowers

There is also a picture by Gauguin, which shows van Gogh at the table painting a picture of sunflowers. This picture is especially interesting, because no photographs exist today of van Gogh painting. There is only this picture to give us an idea of how he worked.

When Gauguin came to Arles to live with van Gogh, however, it was October and the sunflowers had long since faded. So Gauguin could not have watched him painting the sunflowers. He had to use his imagination.

14

Do the two pictures of chairs tell us anything about the friendship between van Gogh and Gauguin? They are almost like portraits, because the chairs show how van Gogh saw himself and his friend. They show how different they were.

Van Gogh's chair stands in a bright room on a stone floor. It is a plain chair, just as simple as the box with onions in it, which is on the floor. On the chair there is a pipe and a little tobacco. Van Gogh shows us how he lived in a simple, modest manner, close to nature.

 on the other hand, is more elegant and stands on a fine carpet. This room is darker.

On the chair there is a lighted candle next to two books. Van Gogh thought of Gauguin as a learned, well-read man and wanted to show this in his picture.

There are many self-portraits by van Gogh.

He painted and drew himself about 40 times!
He often wears a suit and then he portrays himself as a well-groomed gentleman.
In other pictures he has a blue smock on and a yellow straw hat on his head (like the one we saw in his bedroom). Then he is the artist, who is painting outside in the warm sun.

Here van Gogh is wearing a warm fur hat. In the background you can see one of the Japanese pictures of women in front of snow-covered mountains, which he had brought with him from Paris. But what is more striking in this picture is the white bandage around his ear.

What had happened?

The friendship between van Gogh and Gauguin seems to have been a difficult one. In his letters to his brother Theo, Vincent had often grumbled about Gauguin. He felt that Gauguin wasn't interested enough in his plans and his art. The two artists often argued and van Gogh often lost his temper and quickly became angry.
At such moments of depression he no longer had full control of his actions and did not really know what he was doing.
One day, after Gauguin and van Gogh had quarrelled again, Gauguin stormed out of the house. Van Gogh had such a fit of rage and became so confused that he cut off a piece of his ear! He had to stay in hospital for a few days and wore this white bandage round his ear, so that the wound could heal.
But that didn't stop him from painting as you can see.

We now leave Arles and visit a little place called Saint-Rémy-de-Provence, which is also in the south of France.

Van Gogh and his doctor decided that the best thing was for him to have treatment for a while and to find some peace.

So he was admitted to the psychiatric institution in Saint-Rémy, where he was given a bedroom and a studio.

On the window-sill of the studio were a few little bottles and there were drawings hanging on the wall. From the window of his studio, van Gogh could see the green of the trees in the garden and the blue of the sky.

When he felt a bit better, van Gogh was allowed to work in the area around the institution. There he painted a picture of the moon and stars: The Starry Night.
Around the stars he painted yellow circles of light and the almost full moon is also surrounded by a shining halo.
In some places the stars are so close to each other, that they form a long, winding spiral like a hurricane rushing through the night.

This is one of the pictures which later made van Gogh so famous. He painted the things around him as he saw them and how they looked according to him. Other people probably don't see rings around the moon or a hurricane of stars. But van Gogh saw all of this and so he painted it too. And that is what makes his art something quite special.

For the people of his time, however, van Gogh's paintings were too unusual. They neither bought his pictures nor were they exhibited. But although he had no success, van Gogh continued to paint in his own style because he neither wanted nor was able to paint differently.

Of course he did not earn any money by doing this. That is why his brother Theo, who always stuck by him, supported him all his life. He gave him money to live on and for the canvases and expensive paints which he needed.

When Vincent felt well enough to leave the psychiatric clinic, he moved to a little village near Paris called Auvers-sur-Oise. If you wanted to visit him there, you had to go to the inn owned by the Ravoux family, where he had rented a room in the attic. The inn in Auvers still exists today. The room in which van Gogh lived is empty now. But you can easily imagine how he lived. It was probably simply furnished just with a bed, a table and a chair. At the table van Gogh would have written the letters to Theo.

Photo: *Auberge Ravoux,* 1890

A famous picture which was painted there shows a man with a white cap.
It is the doctor who treated van Gogh, Dr. Gachet.
Paul-Ferdinand Gachet lived with his daughter Marguerite and his son Paul in
Auvers-sur-Oise.
Van Gogh became friendly with them and in his letters to Theo was full of praise for Gachet, whom he sometimes called "Père Gachet".
In the picture you can't tell at first glance that this man was a doctor. But there is a little clue. Can you see the flower in front of him on the table? It's a foxglove, which can be used to make medicine. So perhaps this flower is there to tell us that the person in the painting is a doctor! Dr. Gachet looks at us calmly, but he seems worried.
Perhaps he is thinking: "Oh Vincent, I know I'm a doctor, but I won't be able to make you completely well."

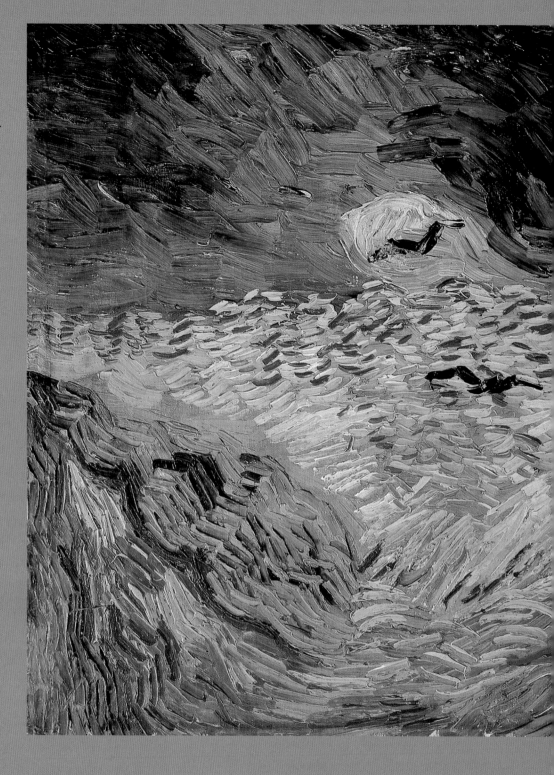

Dr. Gachet had his reasons for thinking this. He knew that van Gogh was still ill and that he often lost control of his senses. The year he had spent in the psychiatric institution had unfortunately not helped very much.

One evening, Dr. Gachet was sent for by the Ravoux family. He was asked to come quickly to the inn, because van Gogh had badly injured himself. In the fields outside Auvers-sur-Oise he had shot himself with a pistol. A few days later he died in the inn, with Theo and Dr. Gachet at his bedside.

We can only begin to understand the problems which van Gogh had to face. Maybe he was unhappy because he hardly ever sold any pictures. His mental health did not improve either. And he might have felt lonely, because, unlike his brother Theo, who lived with his wife Jo and his little son in Paris, he was not married and had no children. In this picture of a wheatfield with crows we can perhaps already detect van Gogh's depression.

The sky is dark and gloomy and the big, black crows fly threateningly over the field.

It is one of the last pictures he painted.

Was he trying to tell us something with this picture? We don't know.

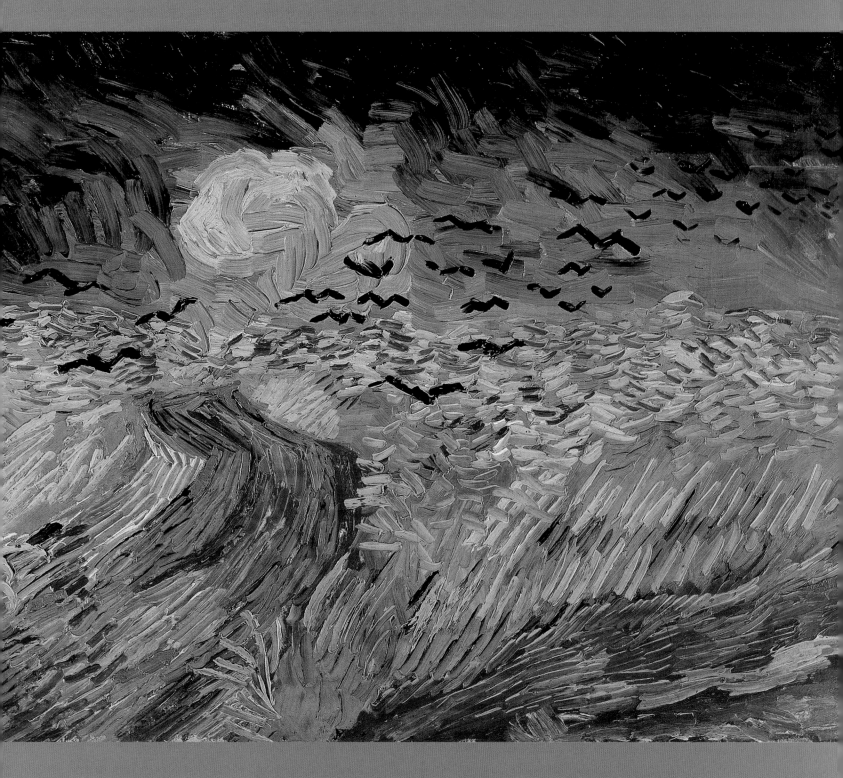

But we do know that on that night an extraordinary artist died, who, although he had little success during his lifetime, is admired today by people throughout the world.

Today millions are paid for the pictures of this headstrong painter. His works are carefully preserved in museums and people come from far away to see them.

If van Gogh were able to visit these museums, he would never believe his eyes!

Vincent van Gogh's pictures.

After van Gogh's death, Theo took all his brother's pictures to his own home. When Theo died himself just six months later, his wife Jo Bonger kept most of the pictures and also carefully preserved the drawings, illustrations and letters, together with the Japanese prints and the paintings by other artists, which Vincent and Theo had collected. Later, Theo van Gogh's son built a museum for them in the Dutch city of Amsterdam. It was called the Van Gogh Museum and was opened in 1973. Of course it is not possible to see all of Vincent van Gogh's works there any more because many pictures have been sold or given away and are now scattered throughout the world. But in the Van Gogh Museum today, there is the largest collection of Vincent van Gogh's works of art in the world. Every day thousands of people come to Amsterdam to admire the famous pictures of the great artist.

The pictures in this book:

Front Cover
The Yellow House (The Street), (see page 8)
Self-Portrait as a Painter (detail), (see page 3)
Back Cover.
Portrait of Dr. Gachet (see page 25)
Title Page
The Bedroom (see page 9)
Page 3
Self-Portrait as a Painter, 1888.
Oil on canvas, 65 x 50.5 cm.
Amsterdam, Van Gogh Museum.
Vincent van Gogh Foundation.
Page 4
Study for The Potato Eaters, 1885.
Drawing, 20 x 33 cm. Amsterdam, Van Gogh Museum. Vincent van Gogh Foundation.
Page 4/5
The Potato Eaters, 1885.
Oil on canvas, 82 x 114 cm.

Amsterdam, Van Gogh Museum.
Vincent van Gogh Foundation.
Page 6
Theo van Gogh, 1888.
Photograph: Amsterdam, Van Gogh Museum.
Vincent van Gogh Foundation.
Page 7
Portrait of Père Tanguy, 1887.
Oil on canvas, 92 x 75 cm.
Paris, Musée Rodin.
Page 8
The Yellow House (The Street), 1888.
Oil on canvas, 76 x 94 cm.
Amsterdam, Van Gogh Museum.
Vincent van Gogh Foundation.
Page 9
The Bedroom, 1888.
Oil on canvas, 79 x 90 cm.
Amsterdam, Van Gogh Museum.
Vincent van Gogh Foundation.
Page 10
Portrait of Joseph Roulin, 1889.
Oil on canvas, 64 x 54.5 cm.
New York, The Museum of Modern Art.
Page 11
Portrait of Augustine Roulin (La Berceuse), 1889. Oil on canvas, 92 x 73 cm.
Otterlo, Kröller-Müller Museum.
Page 12
The Pont de Langlois, (The Bridge near Arles) 1888. Oil on canvas, 54 x 65 cm.
Otterlo, Kröller-Müller Museum.
Page 13
The Café Terrace at Night, 1888.
Oil on canvas, 81 x 61.5 cm.
Otterlo, Kröller-Müller Museum.
Page 14 left
Sunflowers, 1889.
Oil on canvas, 73 x 58 cm.
USA, Private collection.
Page 14 centre
Sunflowers, 1888.
Oil on canvas, 93 x 73 cm.
London, National Gallery.
Page 14 right
Sunflowers, 1888. Oil on canvas, 91 x 71 cm.
Munich, Bayrische Staatsgemäldesammlungen, Neue Pinakothek.

Page 14 bottom
Paul Gauguin, Portrait of van Gogh Painting Sunflowers, 1888. Oil on canvas, 73 x 91 cm.
Amsterdam, Van Gogh Museum.
Vincent van Gogh Foundation.
Page 15
Sunflowers, 1889.
Oil on canvas, 95 x 73 cm.
Amsterdam, Van Gogh Museum.
Vincent van Gogh Foundation.
Page 16
Van Gogh's Chair,1888-1889.
Oil on canvas, 93 x 73.5 cm.
London, National Gallery.
Page 17
Gauguin's Chair, 1888.
Oil on canvas, 90.5 x 72 cm.
Amsterdam, Van Gogh Museum.
Vincent van Gogh Foundation.
Page 19
Self-Portrait with Bandaged Ear, 1889.
Oil on canvas, 60 x 49 cm.
London, Courtauld Institute Galleries.
Page 21
Window of van Gogh's Studio in Saint-Rémy, 1889. Pastel and gouache, 62 x 47.6 cm.
Amsterdam, Van Gogh Museum.
Vincent van Gogh Foundation.
Page 22/23
The Starry Night, 1889.
Oil on canvas, 73 x 92 cm. New York, The Museum of Modern Art.
Page 24
Auberge Ravoux, Auvers-sur-Oise, 1890.
Photograph: Amsterdam, Van Gogh Museum.
Vincent van Gogh Foundation.
Page 25
Portrait of Dr. Gachet, 1890. Oil on canvas, 67 x 56 cm. Tokyo, Private collection.
Page 26/27
Wheatfield with Crows, 1890.
Oil on canvas, 50.5 x 100.5 cm.
Amsterdam, Van Gogh Museum.
Vincent van Gogh Foundation.
Page 29
The Church at Auvers, 1890.
Oil on canvas, 94 x 74 cm.
Paris, Musée d'Orsay.

Text by **Caroline Breunesse**
Translated from the German by
Catherine McCreadie

Library of Congress Cataloging-in-Publication Data available.

Prestel books are available worldwide. Please contact your nearest bookseller or write to either of the following addresses for information concerning your local distributor:

Prestel-Verlag
Mandlstrasse 26, D-80802 Munich
Tel. (+49-89) 381709-0 Fax (+49-89) 381709-35
and 16 West 22nd Street
New York, NY 10010, USA
Tel. (212) 627-8199, Fax (212) 627-9866

Edited by Christopher Wynne
Designed by Maja Thorn
Lithography by Mega-Satz-Service, Berlin
Printed by Aumüller Druck KG, Regensburg
Bound by MIB Conzella, Pfarrkirchen

Printed using ecologically-safe ink
on acid-free paper
Printed in Germany

ISBN 3-7913-1876-4